Summary of

The Four Agreements:

By: Don Miguel Ruiz

Proudly Brought to you by:

Text Copyright © Readtrepreneur

Legal & Disclaimer

Upon using the information contained in this book, you agree to hold harmless the Author from and against any damages, costs, and expenses, including any legal fees potentially resulting from the application of any of the information provided by this guide. This disclaimer applies to any damages or injury caused by the use and application, whether directly or indirectly, of any advice or information presented, whether for breach of contract, tort, negligence, personal injury, criminal intent, or under any other cause of action.

You agree to accept all risks of using the information presented inside this book. You need to consult a professional medical practitioner in order to ensure you are both able and healthy enough to participate in this program.

Table of Contents

The Book at a Glance

Many years ago in southern Mexico, the Toltec, who were a group of artists and scientists, explored and protected the practices and spiritual knowledge of their ancestors. There were the students and the masters, all of them gathering together at one special place in the city.

Over the years, European invasion took place and a few apprentices misused their power. This forced the masters to keep the ancestral knowledge a secret. It was crucial to safeguard the knowledge to stop those who are unworthy of it from using it for selfish reasons.

Fortunately, as the next generations came, the wisdom has been essentially returned to the populace. Don

Miguel Ruiz, who was known to come from a lineage of masters, has been led to impart the Toltec ideologies. These beliefs do not only embrace the spirit, but are also truthfully pronounced as a means of living, in which love and happiness are attainable.

The first chapter of this book will enlighten you about certain aspects of life which you are not really aware of. As children, we were taught so many things, and most of them are based on the beliefs of the people around us. Our parents and teachers taught us what they believe is the proper way for us to behave in our community. They constantly grab our attention to instill in our hearts and minds all the rules and regulations, which we continue to follow as we grow up.

We weren't really given the chance to choose anything for ourselves. We didn't choose our religion, our moral values, and even our names. We just end up accepting everything that is being handed over to us. There are times when we try to fight against their beliefs and opinions, but since we still don't know a lot of things in life, we tend to lose. As a result, we lose our freedom along the way.

There are four new agreements that can help you take back your freedom. These agreements can help you get rid of the old ones and transform your life in a more positive way. The second chapter of this book will introduce you to the first agreement, which is about being impeccable with your word. Sometimes, we tend to throw words at others without really thinking things through. If you make this agreement, you'll be able to use your words with better intentions.

The third chapter is about not taking things personally. We often think about ourselves first in every situation, but not everything is about us. You don't have to prove yourself and be right all the time. Rather, accept that each of us has different beliefs and views about the world. It's an important agreement that you have to make.

Don't make a habit of coming up with immediate assumptions. It's what the fourth chapter of this book will tell you. If you seem doubtful about certain things, it's better to make some clarifications. Otherwise, you might just end up messing things up even more.

To succeed with the first three agreements, you must do your best no matter what. This will be further discussed in the fifth chapter of this book. Nothing can be achieved if we just sit around waiting for things to happen. We can't change our lives if we don't do something about it. Great results come from giving the best of what you have.

Finally, the sixth and seventh chapters of this book will help you better understand the true meaning of freedom by means of breaking your old agreements. We always keep searching for ways to be free and to live our own lives. We form this perfect image, but we can never live up to it. The truth is that no one is perfect and no one can be perfect. Nothing in life is perfect.

It takes a lot of courage to accept ourselves. It also takes a lot of bravery to challenge our beliefs. With all the knowledge that we've accumulated over the years, we can easily choose to do the right thing. However, the problem is that what is right for you may not seem right for others. We all have different thoughts and opinions about things because we all grew up in different ways.

There are numerous agreements we made in our lives as we were growing up, but the agreements we made with ourselves are the most significant ones. They can either set us free and lead us to a path towards happiness or put us in a state of misery. If you seek a life full of enjoyment and satisfaction, you need to break your old agreements that stem from fear. You must take control over your own life.

You no longer have to suffer because of the beliefs that are keeping you from living your life the way you want to. You can create new habits and live a much better life. Everything is within you. Everything is possible. You just have to choose to make the right agreements.

1: Domestication and the Dream of the Planet

You are always dreaming. People are constantly dreaming. The mind's primary function is to dream. It dreams every hour of every day. It dreams when you're asleep and even when you're awake.

Before we came into this world, people before us have already created an outside dream. This is referred to as the society's dream. It is a shared dream made of numerous smaller and personal dreams. All together, they form a family's dream, a community's dream, a city's dream, a country's dream, and the entire humanity's dream. It contains all of the rules, laws, beliefs, religions, and different cultures of society, as well as its schools, governments, holidays, and societal events.

When we were born, the ability to dream is already within us. People prior to our existence have their own ways of teaching us to dream exactly how society dreams. They catch our attention and instill all these rules into our mind.

Attention is what allows us to distinguish and focus on the things that we wish to understand. We can recognize a lot of things all at the same time, but we have the ability to grasp anything we like and concentrate solely on it. The adults persistently grab our attention and fill our minds with various information, repeating them until we learn them by heart. We were taught what they believe is the proper way to behave, what's right and wrong, what's good and bad, and what's acceptable and what's not.

We also learned how to get other people's attention and we become extremely competitive in terms of seeking it. Children compete against each other to make their parents, friends, and teachers notice them. This certain need becomes so strong that we carry it into adulthood.

Our society teaches us everything we need to know, starting with our language. It is through language that people are able to understand and communicate with one another. Each word and each letter becomes an agreement.

We weren't given the chance to choose what specific language we want to speak. We didn't choose our moral values or religion. We didn't have the option of whether or not to accept and believe what others tell us. We weren't even given the chance to pick a name for ourselves.

Because we were just little kids, we were prone to agree with every piece of information that the adults presented to us. It is through agreement that we're able to keep all of the information. We developed a certain faith right at the moment when we agreed and believed in something unconditionally.

It's easy for children to trust what the adults say. There may be times when we tried to defy them, but we didn't have enough strength to defend the things we want. We always ended up losing the argument and surrendering to their beliefs.

This process is called human domestication, where youngsters are being taught to live and dream in a certain way. We receive every piece of advice and guidance that eventually forms our entire belief system.

3

We learned how to judge ourselves and others.

Children are normally trained using the system of reward and punishment. Everytime we follow the rules, a reward awaits, but whenever we disobey the rules, punishment is what we get. Because of this, we learned to become afraid of receiving punishments and we also became afraid when we don't receive any reward. We needed to get the attention of others to gain rewards.

As a result, we often do anything that other people command us to do in exchange for recognition. We pretend to be someone we're not in order to be accepted by others and to be considered desirable by somebody else. Rejection becomes a frightening situation.

We lose our true nature in the process of domestication. Once we grow up and begin to understand the world around us, we learn how to say "no." We defy society because we want to take back our freedom.

At some point, the way we were raised was so intense that we don't need other people anymore to teach us what to do. We acquire enough knowledge to learn on our own. We discipline ourselves when we believe we've violated the rules and we give ourselves rewards for abiding by the rules.

Our belief system is our personal truth that governs our mind. Our judgments are all based on our belief system, even if they tend to challenge our innermost nature. There's a part of our mind that constantly evaluates everything and everyone. There's also another part that receives all the judgments and carries the guilt, blame, and shame.

Your belief system makes you fear anything that goes against it. Whatever it is that makes you question your beliefs will certainly bring you a sense of insecurity. This is the main reason why it's necessary to have the courage to argue regarding our beliefs.

While the government controls society, our own belief system controls our individual dream. We both have the judge, which is the part who rules, and the victim, which is the part that endures the guilt and penalty. However, true justice means paying just once for every mistake that we commit, while true injustice means paying countless times for every mistake made.

Humans are the only creatures that pay numerous times for the very same mistake. We commit an error, assess ourselves, prove that we're guilty and we end up punishing ourselves. Whenever our mistakes are brought back to mind, we still punish ourselves repeatedly.

In our society, people normally suffer, feel anxious, and create all kinds of emotional dramas. The world becomes a difficult place to settle in due to the fear that governs it. We witness human suffering, injustice, violence, addictions, hatred, and revenge all around the world.

Our society nowadays can be compared to hell, which has been described and made known by various religions throughout the world. Hell is said to be a place where there is endless pain, fear, and punishment. People can bring us down to that dark place if we let them. However, it's also possible to escape from that nightmare. We can try to obtain and enjoy a good life.

Humanity has always been seeking beauty, justice, and truth. The search never stops, but what we don't realize is that everything already exists within us. The problem is that we don't have the eyes to see the truth because of the distressing beliefs and agreements that are clouding our minds. We are blinded from seeing the truth. Every false belief prevents us from seeing things clearly. We only rely on the things we believe in, but they only lead us towards a path of pain and suffering.

The mind is a vision where thousands of people talk simultaneously and no one understands what others are trying to say. We can't see the real us and we're not aware that we're being imprisoned. This is exactly why people struggle with life. Their biggest fear is to be truly alive. We're afraid to go out, take risks, and show our true character. We became comfortable living our lives while continuously attempting to please other people.

We create something which we believe is the perfect image and try to live up to it. We form an ideal image of ourselves that is acceptable to the community. Still, this particular image isn't real. We can never be perfect. No one can ever be perfect.

We have the tendency to reject ourselves when we

1: DOMESTICATION AND THE DREAM OF THE PLANET

realize that we're an imperfect human being. We're not contented with ourselves because we're nothing like the perfect image that we visualize in our head. We're not what we're meant to be and we can't forgive ourselves for it. We hide our true selves and put on these social masks so others won't notice. We also judge others based on our idea of perfection. Of course, they obviously fail to meet our expectations as well.

Due to our imperfections, we always seem to end up punishing ourselves. Many people abuse themselves and they even find ways to use others to abuse them. How much you abuse yourself is exactly how much you can tolerate other people's abuse towards you.

It's ironic that we have this desire to be loved and accepted by other people, but we can't love and accept ourselves. If you don't want to experience self-abuse, you need to learn to love who you are. Drop that perfect image you have in mind. It's the only way you can avoid self-rejection. If you can embrace your own imperfections, then you'll be able to embrace others and accept them for who they really are.

Throughout our lives, we've made countless agreements with ourselves, with others, with the society, and even with God. Still, those agreements that you established with yourself are the most essential ones. Together, they form your personality.

We have plenty of agreements that only bring chaos and suffering in our lives. You need to be brave enough to break your old agreements that are based on fear in order to attain a life that's filled with joy and love.

All you need are four powerful agreements to help you overcome your old habits that set your life in fear and drain all of your energy. Adopting these agreements will provide you with sufficient personal power so you'll be able to transform your whole belief system. Your life can become quite remarkable. There will be no more reason to stay in hell. The power to create heaven is within your reach.

2: <u>THE FIRST AGREEMENT</u>

Be Impeccable with Your Word

This is considered to be the most significant agreement, but also the hardest one to fulfill. Although it sounds quite simple, it is indeed a powerful agreement. It will help you go beyond the existence of the so-called "heaven on earth."

You have the power to create with your word. It's a gift that God has given directly to you. Your abilities can be expressed by means of your word. Everything is reflected through your words, especially who you are and what you think and feel.

The word isn't merely a written sign or a sound, but rather a force that allows you to communicate, express, think, and create different life circumstances. It's a very powerful instrument entrusted to humans. You can either form a wonderful dream or destroy the things around you. It can either give you freedom, or imprison you. It all depends upon how you use it. It's regarded as pure magic, but it becomes black magic when you misuse its power.

The mind is similar to a fruitful land where different seeds are constantly being planted. Your ideas, opinions, and concepts are the seeds. When you plant them in your mind, they grow. It's important to set the mind up to collect those seeds that stem from love.

We must recognize the kind of power that our words possess. When we were kids, our friends and family members offered us their opinions without really thinking about it. We immediately believed everything they told us, like when we were told that we were not excellent in sports, any form of art, or math. We carry all these things with us. These demeaning remarks made us live in fear.

By grabbing our attention, other people's words can easily enter our heads and transform our beliefs in either a good or hurtful way. For instance, when someone catches your attention and tells you that you're a foolish person and you think it's true, that agreement will most likely be strengthened and become stronger.

In terms of the meaning of impeccability, the word refers to having no sin. Various religions discuss the concept of sin. It's something you do that creates conflict with your own self. You deny yourself whenever you blame or judge yourself for something you've done wrong. Being impeccable isn't rejecting yourself. It's when you're responsible for your behavior without the need to condemn yourself.

When you reject yourself, that's when sin begins. It's a major sin that you could possibly commit. Self-rejection only leads to destruction, while impeccability promotes life.

If you love yourself and you show that love through your interactions with others, then you're using your word in an impeccable manner. Your selfless actions create a similar reaction. The right way to use your energy is to stay true to your words. You direct your words toward love and truth. When you incorporate and improve this agreement in your life, you'll be able to eliminate every emotional pain inside you and reflect your truth. This is certainly a difficult thing to maintain since we have the habit of lying when we communicate with others and we also tend to lie to ourselves.

We often use our words to blame others, to curse, and destroy. We use our power to express hate, anger, resentment, and jealousy. Chaos begins with our words. We breed hatred among nations, races, people, and families. If we fall down, we drag others down with us and remain in a fearful and confused state.

Every time we listen to other people's opinion and trust what they say, we come up with an agreement that eventually adds up to our established beliefs. People who throw black magic directly at us aren't usually aware of what they're doing, that's why we need to forgive them.

Sometimes, people's perspectives in life are harmful spells that are hard to break. Building another agreement grounded from truth is the only way to defeat them. The truth holds the power that can break these hurtful spells and free us from all the pain and sorrow. It's extremely important when it comes to the proper usage of words.

When you look at the day-to-day interactions of people, we tend to say unkind words to one another countless times. This form of communication is commonly known as gossip and it has turned into the worst kind of wicked black magic.

Gossiping is something we learned by agreement. During our childhood, we constantly hear adults gossiping and frankly giving their thoughts and sentiments regarding other people. They always have something to say, even for those they don't know so well. We believed that this is just how people normally communicate.

Today in our society, gossiping has already become an important means of communication. We feel like we've established a close relationship with other people whenever we tell tales. Somehow, it brings us a sense of relief when we see another person feel bad the same way we do.

Gossip works like a computer virus, which is a part of the computer language that's made up of the same components as every other computer code, but with the intention to harm the system. It's usually installed into a computer program without you knowing it. Then all of a sudden, your computer doesn't seem to work right or it no longer functions at all.

14

In the same way, every piece of wrong information can ruin people's communication. People often resort to spreading gossip to one another to escape confusion and find relief. Gossiping is like inserting some computer viruses into each other's mind. It makes you think less clearly. Imagine what it would be like if this scheme goes on and on among people all over the world. The world would be full of people who send and receive information through clogged circuits.

Even your own opinion is merely considered as based on your feelings and sentiments. It's not entirely true. Every opinion you give stems from your own dream, beliefs, and ego. We tend to create hatred and then pass it on to others to validate our personal views.

We must understand what our words can do. Recognizing this first agreement makes you envision all the positive transformations that can take place in life. First, in how you properly treat yourself, and second, in how you act towards other people, particularly the ones you love dearly.

If we learn how to be impeccable with our word, we'll

be able to get rid of all the emotional poison and clear our minds. Our communication in terms of personal relations will improve. If you remain impeccable with your word, you make yourself immune from any negative spell that others cast at you. Your mind doesn't become this fertile ground that collects seeds of black magic. It becomes fertile only for those that stem from love. These are the kinds of seeds that you should nurture and allow to grow inside your mind. It'll eventually produce more love and replace the seeds that come from fear.

The sincerity and nature of your words will reflect the love you have for yourself. Your words can tell how good or happy you feel or that you're at peace with yourself. You can go beyond the world of darkness when you make this agreement a part of your life. You'll obtain happiness and freedom.

Always remember to use your word for good intentions. Use the power of your word to spread love to others. Lift yourself up by knowing how great and wonderful you are. See this as an opportunity to break those small agreements that bring suffering and chaos. You can

16

transform your entire life by being impeccable with your word. It can direct your path towards success, abundance, and personal freedom. You'll no longer live in fear, but rather in pure love and happiness.

3: <u>THE SECOND AGREEMENT</u>

Don't Take Anything Personally

Whatever it is that happens in your life, don't think about it too hard. If someone sees you and says you're stupid, but that person doesn't really know you, what they state has nothing to do with you. It's about him and not you. If you let yourself ponder on it, maybe you think it's true.

You usually take things personally seeing that you completely agree with what was stated. The moment you accept other people's opinion, you trap yourself in a nightmare. This is referred to as personal importance. It's the highest form of selfishness since you assume that every single thing is about you. You believe that you're responsible for a whole lot of things.

Whatever it is that people do, it has nothing to do with you. It's about themselves. Every one of us lives in our own mind and in our personal dream. Our world is entirely different from the world others are living in. When we take things personally, we think other people understand our world. We also attempt to force ourselves into their world.

When a particular situation seems very personal, or if other people throw insults at you, it's still not about you. People say what they want to say and do what they want to do based on their own agreements in life. Their opinions come from the way they were raised and the things that were taught to them.

When someone gives a remark, they are just behaving according to their own opinions, beliefs, and feelings. If that person tries to offer you spite, it only becomes your own personal spite if you believe it. It's easy to grab someone's attention with just a single opinion and give them any negative judgment. Consider it a gift if you become immune to these kinds of bitterness in life.

It upsets you when you're very sensitive to the words and actions of others, so you end up defending your views, which leads to conflicts. You make a big deal out of small things because you think you're right and what everybody else says is wrong. But no matter what you feel, say, or do, it only reflects the agreements that you have made in your life. Your problem isn't other people's problem. You have a different way of seeing the world. It's your own movie or picture that you create inside your head.

Your thoughts and feelings are unique to you. They are your personal truths. If you're angry, you're only taking on yourself. You just make other people a great excuse to be angry. You're furious because you're actually afraid of something.

Negative emotions have no place in your life if you choose to love and abandon fear. You'll have that sense of delight towards everything. You feel happy with everything and you love everything because you love yourself. You're happy, contented, and at peace with your life. Your agreements make you happy. Everything around you becomes great.

Your opinions about yourself aren't entirely true as well. Sometimes, the mind speaks to itself. It's capable of hearing information coming from other outside realms.

You even wonder where that certain voice is coming from when you try to listen to it.

The mind usually sees and perceives reality with your two eyes, but it can also see in the absence of the eyes. It doesn't dwell in only one dimension. Still, we can choose whether to listen and believe in the voices in our heads or ignore them. Also, we can choose whether or not to accept and agree with what society tells us.

The mind both listens and talks to itself. When thousands of voices are trying to speak all at once, then that's a serious problem. It's like being in a marketplace where countless people simultaneously talk and trade. Every one of them has varying feelings and opinions. Every one of them differs in perspective. Every agreement isn't essentially compatible with one another. Some are in conflict and clash with other agreements. This is why people are always unsure of the things they want. They disagree with their own selves because some parts of their mind wish for one thing, and the other parts wish for another different thing.

There are some parts that are opposed to a particular thought or action, while other parts support every single idea. This creates an internal struggle. The only way you can unveil every conflict in your mind and bring order to the confusion is to become aware of all your agreements in life.

You'll only make yourself suffer when you take things personally. People seem to be obsessed with suffering at varying levels and degrees. They even do other people a favor by helping them suffer even more. If you want to abuse yourself, it becomes easy for others to abuse you as well.

Don't expect that people will always be honest with you because they tend to be dishonest with themselves. Trust yourself instead and make a choice of whether or not to trust what other people tell you.

When you see people the way they are and you don't easily take into heart the things they tell you, you won't end up getting upset. You'll find that it's okay if they lie about something because you know they're not perfect, and trying to remove someone's social mask can be distressing. However, if their actions don't match their words, then you're just being dishonest with yourself if you continue to believe them. It'll save you from a great deal of emotional heartbreak if you remain honest with yourself.

Think of it as a gift when someone who doesn't treat you right walks out of your life. Everyone deserves some respect and love. Even though it may hurt at first, you heart will find a way to heal. You'll see that you can trust yourself when it comes to doing the right thing. You don't have to rely on others. There are plenty of ways to set yourself free from constant suffering.

Once you learn how not to take things personally, you'll be able to break your bad habits that cause unnecessary pain. Never think that you're responsible for other people's actions. You are responsible for yours. As soon as you realize this, you can never be bothered by the thoughtless opinions and actions people direct at you.

You'll be free to go anywhere with a fully open heart and there's nothing that can upset or hurt you. You'll no longer be afraid of rejection or criticisms. You can do what you feel in your heart that's right and experience genuine happiness and peace regardless of how messy the world can be.

4: <u>THE THIRD AGREEMENT</u>

Don't Make Assumptions

Oftentimes, we tend to assume many different things. We think they're true and this can actually cause real problems. We come up with all kinds of assumptions, misunderstand things, take them personally, and end up making unnecessary drama in life.

We seem to be too scared to clear things up, this is why we formulate guesses and believe we're right about them. We even defend them and make sure that others get it wrong. Assumptions only bring suffering. Just ask questions. It's always a better option.

The mind produces chaos, making us misunderstand or misinterpret a lot of things. We don't clearly see things as they are. We only notice what we wish to notice and even form things out of our imaginations. When we can't understand certain things, we assume that it means something and we become disappointed when it's not what we have expected at all.

When it comes to relationships, our assumptions usually cause problems. We often assume that there's no need to say anything because our life partners know exactly what we're thinking. They are aware of the things we want, and they'll do everything we want. If they fail, we feel hurt. Making assumptions only result in several arguments, misunderstandings and difficulties.

Our mind works in a very interesting way. We have this constant need to explain, justify, and figure out everything just to feel secure. The mind simply can't explain everything, which is why we come up with assumptions. It doesn't matter if we get the right answers because the answers alone put us out of harm's way.

Making assumptions satisfy our demand to be informed and it gives us no reason to communicate. We assume even when we hear things that we can't quite comprehend because we're afraid to raise questions.

We usually make assumptions quickly and unconsciously because we have agreed that this is an acceptable form of communication. We tend to believe in something so hard that we even end up ruining our relationships just to support our own perspective.

We think that other people view life the same way as we do, that's why we hide our true selves when we're surrounded by other people. We believe that they'll judge us or blame us like we do with ourselves. We reject ourselves even before we get rejected by others.

We also tend to assume a lot about ourselves. We either underestimate or overestimate our abilities because we haven't really taken some time to look at ourselves, ask questions, and answer them. Maybe it's time to be more truthful about the things we really want.

When you like someone and enter into a kind of special relationship, you often explain several things that you like about that person. You may even assume that when you love that person, it'll change him or her. However, people change not because of you, but because it's what they want to do. Love isn't meant to be justified. When you really love someone, you'll accept him or her without forcing them to change. If you want them to change, perhaps you don't really love them at all. It's better to find someone that you can fully accept regardless of their flaws. That person should also do the same with you.

Be who you really are. There's no need to pretend to be someone you're not. If others love you, then it's great. If they don't like you, then it's okay. It may not sound idealistic, but you should always make your agreements with other people perfectly clear.

Ask questions. It's the only way to stop yourself from drawing up all kinds of assumptions. If something doesn't make sense to you, don't be afraid to ask until everything becomes clear. Don't even assume that you know everything about a certain situation.

Speak up and ask for something that you want. You are entitled to ask, but everyone is also entitled to say yes or no. Having clear communication will transform your relationships in a positive way. If we can achieve this kind of interaction, violence and misunderstandings could be avoided.

Yet, it's really a hard thing to do because we're used to doing the opposite. We're not even aware of all the habits we have. Take the first step of recognizing your habits and take into heart the significance of this third agreement. However, it's not enough to merely understand it. What's more important is doing something about it. If you take action repeatedly, you'll nurture a good seed and form a strong foundation for new habits to develop. Practice it over and over again until it becomes your second nature.

Magic happens when you start changing things in life for the better. Everything will appear easy to you because the spirit moves willingly inside you. It's the knowledge of spirit, intent, gratitude, love, and life. It's what leads you towards having personal freedom.

5: <u>THE FOURTH AGREEMENT</u>

Always Do Your Best

This fourth agreement is about taking action for all the previous agreements. It helps every one of them to become our deep-seated habits.

No matter what happens in life, make sure that you always put your best effort in anything you do. However, remember that your finest performance may not always be the same. Everything is constantly changing. There will be days when you'll be at your best and days when you'll be at your worst. Your capacity during the morning period when you're recharged and energized will be superior unlike when you come home feeling tired at night. You'll be in top shape when you're healthy compared to when you're sick. You give your best when you're feeling great and happy, unlike when you're feeling sad or angry.

Your moods can change daily. It can also change from

time to time. Just don't let it stop you from working on these new agreements. You'll eventually become better at sticking with them.

It doesn't matter whether your work is excellent or not, just always do your best. Still, don't be too hard on yourself. You'll only end up wasting your energy. You don't have to wear yourself out all the time because you might just end up accomplishing your goal longer than usual. But don't let yourself do less since that would only lead to guilt, frustrations, and regrets.

You'll have no reason to judge yourself if you always give your best shot. It stops you from feeling guilty, blaming yourself or even punishing yourself. You don't exist just to experience suffering. You're here to experience joy in your life, to love and live happily. You don't even have to go meditating for several hours to attain peace and happiness. Doing your best even in just a short amount of time is enough for you to appreciate life.

If you give everything you've got, you'll definitely be productive and you'll feel good about yourself because you know you didn't settle for anything less. It's all about the action because you take pleasure in what you do, not because it comes with a reward.

Many people work hard every single day and look forward to payday. They can't wait for the weekend to arrive. They only work because of the reward and they force themselves to endure their work days, which appears to be a lot difficult. They work tirelessly not out of love, but because it's necessary. Working is how they are able to pay their bills, or provide for their family. Eventually, all these frustrations start to surface and by the time they receive their salary, they're miserable and they hate their life.

On the contrary, if you work hard because you love what you do whether there's a reward or not, you'll get to experience more fun in life. You wouldn't feel like as if you're working because what you do makes you happy. You give everything you can at your job because it's what you want or choose to do, not because you're trying to be nice to get other people to like you. Although rewards may come, you don't spend time thinking about them. You might even get more than what you expected. More importantly, you live with no regrets. This is why it's essential to keep this agreement.

As you build this habit and make it a part of your daily life, you'll learn to love and accept yourself. You just have to realize that you may make some mistakes, but you can learn from them. One way to do this is to keep on practicing.

To live fully is to take action. You refuse to live if you remain inactive. For instance, you choose to sit on the couch all day watching television because you're scared to live, take risks, and express who you really are. Even though your mind has all of these great ideas, it wouldn't matter unless you go out and turn them into a reality. Taking action is how you'll be able to gain your desired outcomes.

Don't be afraid to explore and take risks. Go and show people the things that you dream about. Your dream is worth manifesting. Think of it as sharing your goals with the world rather than trying to impose your dreams on other people.

Every time you give your best, you give back to God.

Leaving the past behind and learning to live in the present is a great way to give Him thanks. There's no need to wish things differently. You simply enjoy being alive and appreciate every opportunity that comes.

You have the freedom to love and be happy. You're free to share your love and happiness with others. Don't let life pass you by because it's like letting God just pass through you. Your mere existence shows that God truly exists. Your existence shows that life and spirit exists.

You don't have to prove anything at all, or know everything. All you need to do is live your life to the fullest. You're free to be yourself and your best self comes from doing your best. There's no need for some great knowledge or philosophical ideas. You don't have to please others. Your divine nature is manifested through your life and love.

You can succeed with the other agreements if you work hard to achieve them. After some time, you're less likely to go back to your old habits. Through constant practice, you'll be able to master the art of transformation. Repetition is how we learned everything we now know in life. Doing it makes all the difference.

You'll soon be able to find what you're looking for if you give your full self in seeking personal freedom and self-love. Get up and experience humanity. Keep in mind that God manifests through you. You honor Him with every word you say and every action you take. You give glory to Him with your entire being.

When you give importance to the meaning of these agreements and adopt them, there's no doubt that you'll have a better and more beautiful life. You take your power back and regain control over your own life. Once they're deeply established in your inner being, you can transform your nightmare into your personal heaven.

Life can present you with a lot of challenges and obstacles throughout your journey. A strong will is what you'll need to stick to these new agreements. Don't let anything stop you from succeeding. It's where your life, freedom, and happiness lie. It's how you can finally escape suffering.

There will be times when you need to get a bit hard on yourself. If you fail, just keep going. It will eventually become a lot easier. Don't judge yourself if you stumble along the way. You can always stand up and start again.

Don't worry about the days to come. Focus on the present moment. Allow your self-respect and love to grow continually. Delight in every single day of your life. It's never too late start a new kind of dream.

6: <u>THE TOLTEC PATH TO FREEDOM</u>

Breaking Old Agreements

Everyone wants to be free. Throughout the world, several people, races, and countries keep on fighting for their freedom. However, we still remain prisoners of life because we're not entirely free. Real freedom is about having an unrestrained spirit. It's about having the right to express who we really are.

We often blame our religion, our parents, our school, the government, and even God because we feel trapped. Yet, we are actually the ones who stop ourselves from becoming free. People tend to say that they have lost their freedom when they got married, but when they break up with their partner, they still aren't free. We were once free people, but we've forgotten the true meaning of freedom.

When we look at a child, we see a person who's free.

Children normally do whatever they want to do. They're wild. They always throw this big smile because they're having so much fun while playing and trying to explore the world around them. They're only scared when they get hurt or when they feel hungry. Yet, they don't think about the future or the past. They just live and enjoy the present.

Children are not scared to express their true feelings. They're very loving and they're just receiving love in every direction. This is what a normal person should be like. Our true nature is to just play, be happy, explore, enjoy life, and love everything around us.

Unfortunately, we lose our freedom when we grow up because we have formed a certain belief system that doesn't let us show our true selves. But there's no need to hold your parents accountable for raising you to become like them. They only did their best to teach you what they have learned while they were growing up.

Deep inside, you're still that little kid. That little kid comes out every time you play, write, paint, or express yourself in any way. Whenever your true character comes out, that's when you usually have the best moments of your life.

However, all these responsibilities began to emerge and they changed everything. We are constantly reminded to excel in school and to go to work and earn money. Every time we remember our responsibilities, our face goes back to being serious.

To be who we really are is the kind of freedom that we're searching for. Still, if we take a closer look at what our lives are like, we'll see that we often do things to please other people and we don't even recognize it. To find solutions to any problem, we must first understand the real problem.

You can't change anything if you don't know what's wrong. Your emotional wounds won't heal and you'll just keep on suffering. But there's really no point in letting yourself suffer. You can find ways to transform your life. If you start questioning your belief system, you might be surprised to find that many are just based on lies.

It's important that you understand your personal dream

because it manifests your life. If you don't like your life, you can choose to change it whenever you want to. Dream masters make their life a masterpiece. They make their own choices and they are aware that every choice they make has a consequence.

Becoming a Toltec is a manner of living without leaders and followers and living with your personal truth. They possess a map that helps them escape from domestication and lead them to the pathway of freedom. They believe that your belief system is a parasite that governs your mind and your life.

What we really seek is the freedom to be truly alive and do whatever we want with our lives. We actually have two choices when it comes to this. We can either choose to continue living the same way or be like children who resist and are brave enough to say no.

Many people in Canada, America, and Argentina consider themselves as warriors. A warrior fights against the attack of parasites. However, we don't necessarily have to win the battle, but rather do our very best at all times to have the chance to regain our freedom.

Becoming a warrior provides us with the opportunity to go beyond the society's dream and to change our lives into our personal heaven that exists in our mind. It's a place of love and happiness, where we no longer need to hide our true selves. It's possible to attain heaven in this world. We just need to open our eyes and listen with our ears to realize the truth.

One of the things we can do is to face our fears one at a time. We slowly work our way towards freedom whenever we overcome our fears. We need to be aware of all our beliefs and agreements and find the courage to change them. Remember that you're not a child anymore. As we grow up, our innocence is taken away. It's now up to us to make our own choices. We can believe whatever we want and we can choose to believe in ourselves.

You need to be aware of everything to make your life transformation possible. But you have to focus on the things that you really want to change. Think about all of your beliefs that stem from fear, all those that make you suffer and limit your true potential. Once you have a list of these old agreements, you can begin the process of transformation. You can start by exploring and adopting stronger beliefs, including the four new agreements.

These agreements offer you the chance to put an end to your emotional pain and to live a happier life. These agreements were formed to assist and guide you in breaking your old agreements to obtain personal power and to become a stronger individual. But you need to establish new agreements in exchange of the old agreements that you break.

This journey will really require patience. Don't expect that you'll be able to break all your old agreements in just a single day. The best way to become better at it is to keep on practicing.

Another solution is to cease strengthening the parasite. We must learn to control our emotions, especially the ones that are based on fear. Every day, we wake up with a specific amount of physical, emotional, and mental energy that we consume for the entire day. Don't let your emotions drain all of your energy. Otherwise, there'll be no energy left for you to transform your life or to share with others.

Your emotions dictate how you view the world around you. When you're angry, everything else seems wrong. When you're sad, everything makes you want to cry.

The mind is like infected skin. Each of us has a body that's entirely covered with wounds. Every single wound is contaminated with poison, making us suffer from sadness, anger, envy, and hatred. When someone tries to hurt us, they open a certain wound and we respond according to our thoughts and beliefs about fairness and injustice.

People have this mental illness called fear. The rational mind starts to fail when fear turns out to be far too serious. We can only find a cure once we realize that we are infected with this disease.

Forgiveness is part of the healing process. We must learn to forgive others out of self-love because we want to free ourselves from the torment. We don't have to imprison ourselves with this bitterness. We don't have to abuse or beat ourselves up. Self-acceptance starts right at the moment when you learn to forgive yourself, forgive others, and forgive God. Your wounds would no longer hurt even if someone tries to touch them. This is where real freedom begins.

Most of the time, the problem is that people can't handle their emotions well. They let their emotions control their behavior, not the other way around. As a result, we say several things that we don't really mean or do various things that are against our nature.

That's why it's important to be a warrior. A warrior is aware of himself. A warrior has the ability to control his own behavior and emotions, and to convey these emotions at the proper moment. We must acknowledge that there's a war taking place and that the battles inside our heads demand a warrior's discipline. We must have the discipline and the courage to be who we really are, regardless of the circumstances.

Lastly, the third approach is the commencement of death, where the parasite is killed symbolically, without causing any harm to our actual body. It's a faster solution, but it's harder to execute. Facing death requires a whole lot of courage.

We think of death as our master or teacher. Death

teaches us how to really live our lives to the fullest. We recognize the fact that we could possibly die any time. Thus, we are offered with two choices. We can either suffer because death is inevitable, or we can use every second doing what we love and being happy. This approach teaches us to live like there's no tomorrow. It shows us how to open our hearts and to not be scared of anything.

Your old beliefs and agreements will be gone forever. The parasite in your mind will be completely destroyed. If you survive this, restoration will be the greatest gift you'll ever receive. You'll become like a little kid again, free but no longer innocent. You'll have the freedom to live your life in your own terms. Death wipes out the past and allows us to enjoy the present moment and live our lives in the best way possible.

7: <u>THE NEW DREAM</u>

Heaven on Earth

Ignore the things that people taught you in your entire life. It's time to start creating your own dream. You have the ability to create your own life and you can reshape it whenever you like. It's up to you if you're going to live life in heaven or in hell.

People often imagine what it would be like to live a different life. Imagine having a different pair of eyes and try to view the world in a totally different way. You'll be able to understand and recognize love that is all around you. Even if people seem angry or sad, you can also see the love they're trying to convey. That is a state of complete happiness.

You no longer have a reason to defend your existence. You're free to express who you are without any form of struggle. You live a life where you're not afraid to express your dreams and you're not afraid of what other people might think. What matters is that you truly know what it is that you want. No one can control you and there's no need for you to control others.

Think about what it's like to live without the need to judge others. You don't have to criticize anyone and it would be easy to forgive other people's wrongdoings. You don't need to prove that you're always right and make other people wrong. You show respect to others and to yourself. In return, you gain respect.

Envision a life full of love. You're not scared to love and not be loved by others. Rejection doesn't bother you because it's okay whether people accept you or not. You're not afraid of getting hurt and you can freely walk around this world with an open heart.

Imagine life without the fear of taking risks and exploring life. There's nothing to lose. You're not scared to die and you're certainly not scared to be truly alive. You recognize your imperfections, but you still accept and love yourself despite being imperfect.

It's absolutely possible to live your life this way. You can achieve a state of grace and bliss through love. Love provides happiness. Everywhere you go, you'll be able to perceive love. This kind of life is attainable because there are people who have already done it. They established new agreements and this is why they're living a much happier life. You can live like them as well because you're not entirely different from them.

You'll realize that heaven really exists. As soon as you understand that it's within your reach, you have to put a lot of effort to remain in that place. Many years ago, God's kingdom, a land of love and heaven, was told by Jesus, but no one was prepared to listen to it. Once you receive this special message, you'll find love within yourself.

The world we live in is marvelous and beautiful. Life is easy when you let love direct it. You can love everything and everyone around you. It's your choice. Even if there aren't any reasons for you to love, you still do because it makes you happy. Love brings joy and provides you with a sense of inner peace. Your perception about the world around you changes because of love.

For centuries, people have been seeking happiness. They

work so hard to achieve it. The truth is that your happiness lies in your own hands. It's just that you let your beliefs cloud your judgment. Let go of your old agreements and allow yourself to feel and experience love. Don't let yourself suffer for no reason at all and become comfortable living that way. You only suffer because you want to. There are plenty of excuses to let yourself suffer, but there's never a good intention for it. It's a choice you have to make. You can either choose to be happy or live miserably. You can choose to dwell in heaven or you can choose to stay in hell. Nevertheless, heaven is certainly a better choice.

Prayers

Take some time to close your eyes and let love fill your heart. Breathe deeply and gently as the air starts to fill your lungs. Appreciate the connection and allow yourself to feel the love. Experience the joy of simply breathing because it's what makes you alive. Then pray to our Heavenly Father and feel that strong sense of connection with Him.

DEVOTION FOR FREEDOM AND LOVE

Pray to our Creator to come and be with us and bestow upon us His unconditional love for He is love. He is the only one that prevails in this world. Ask Him to help us become like Him, to love anyone and everything around us without expectations, conditions, or judgment. Seek His guidance so we can learn to accept and love ourselves despite our imperfections.

He is the one who created everything, so we should learn to love His creation, especially human beings. Pray that He helps us love those whom we find difficult to love because every time we reject others, we also reject ourselves, especially Him.

Ask that He cleanses our hearts and removes every emotional pain we have, that He unburdens our minds to prevent any form of judgment so we can experience peace and love.

Make this day a special one. Pray that our Heavenly Father would open our beautiful hearts so we can tell others how much we truly love and appreciate them without feeling scared. Let us offer our whole being to

Him that He may use us to share His love with the world.

Give Him thanks for every opportunity we have to be free to express our true beings. Thank Him for the life he has given us and for everything we have ever needed. Show Him how grateful we are because we get to experience a wonderful mind and body and that His pure love, His abundant spirit, and His radiant light lives inside us.

We must express our love towards our Creator because we're able to love ourselves the same way He loves us. Let us pray that He may continue to retain the peace and love in our hearts so we may exist in love forever.

Conclusion

When we were young, our limited knowledge allowed adults to teach us what they know. They taught us what they believe is right or wrong. They taught us how to behave in certain ways, which they think is correct. They simply passed on to us the same knowledge that people before them passed on to them. We didn't get to choose what we wanted to learn. We form all these beliefs and when others try to challenge them, we feel afraid. As a result, we try to hide our true selves and suffer from fear because we can't live up to society's expectations.

Most of the time, our habits are what cause us to suffer. The good thing is that we can break them. Little by little, we can eliminate them by incorporating the four new and better agreements in our daily lives.

You can start by acknowledging the power of your word. You need to be careful with what you say to other people. Your words can either uplift them or bring them down. You can create a beautiful life or you can destroy the life you already have. This is why gossiping is not an ideal solution towards a better communication. Instead, use your words to spread kindness and goodness. It's a first step to make the world a better place to live in.

Don't believe everything that others tell you. No matter what they say or do, it has nothing to do with you. Their words and actions are based on their own agreements. It's what they have been taught. Each of us live our lives in completely different ways. Our world is different from that of others.

If you don't understand something, find the courage to ask. Also, don't think that you know everything. It's better to have a clear communication than to assume and misinterpret things. Otherwise, it will only lead to a lot of conflicts and misunderstandings in your relationship with other people.

Do your best to adopt these new agreements in your life. It won't be easy at first, but just keep moving forward no matter what happens. You'll become better at applying these positive changes in your life. Just remember not to push yourself too hard. Take it one step at a time. You'll certainly have no regrets and you won't have any reason to judge or punish yourself if you put your best effort into it. What's important is that you're taking action towards improving every aspect of your life.

Since you're already knowledgeable about so many things learned while growing up, it's up to you to change your agreements any time you want to. You can always start a new journey towards happiness and freedom. You can be free to express your true self without that constant fear of being judged or rejected by others. Use your power to create a better world in which you can love yourself, as well as everyone else around you.

It's possible to experience heaven in the midst of hell. There's no reason for you to remain stuck in misery. The world is still a wonderful and beautiful place. Life can be great if you simply choose to do what's best for you. Everything is up to you, so choose to live a life of love and happiness by living the four agreements you learned from this book.

FREE BONUSES

<u>P.S. Is it okay if we overdeliver?</u>

Here at Readtrepreneur Publishing, we believe in overdelivering way beyond our reader's expectations. Is it okay if we overdeliver?

Here's the deal, we're going to give you an extremely condensed PDF summary of the book which you've just read and much more...

What's the catch? We need to trust you... You see, we want to overdeliver and in order for us to do that, we've to trust our reader to keep this bonus a secret to themselves? Why? Because we don't want people to be getting our exclusive PDF summaries even without buying our books itself. Unethical, right?

Ok. Are you ready?

Firstly, remember that your book is code: "**READ98**".

Next, visit this link: <u>http://bit.ly/exclusivepdfs</u>

Everything else will be self explanatory after you've visited: **http://bit.ly/exclusivepdfs**.

We hope you'll enjoy our free bonuses as much as we enjoyed preparing it for you!

CPSIA information can be obtained
at www.ICGtesting.com
Printed in the USA
LVHW092336241019
635296LV00001BA/155/P

9 781646 151974